Raspberry Pi 3:

Step By Step Guide From Beginner To Advanced

by
Leonard Eddison

© Copyright 2017 by Leonard Eddison

All rights reserved.

The follow eBook is reproduced below with the goal of providing information that is as accurate and reliable as possible. Regardless, purchasing this eBook can be seen as consent to the fact that both the publisher and the author of this book are in no way experts on the toPics discussed within and that any recommendations or suggestions that are made herein are for entertainment purposes only. Professionals should be consulted as needed prior to undertaking any of the action endorsed herein.

This declaration is deemed fair and valid by both the American Bar Association and the Committee of Publishers Association and is legally binding throughout the United States.

Furthermore, the transmission, duplication or reproduction of any of the following work including specific information will be considered an illegal act irrespective of if it is done electronically or in print. This extends to creating a secondary or tertiary copy of the work or a recorded copy and is only allowed with express written consent from the Publisher. All additional right reserved.

The information in the following pages is broadly considered to be a truthful and accurate account of facts and as such any inattention, use or misuse of the information in question by the reader will render any resulting actions solely under their purview. There are no scenarios in which the publisher or the original author of this work can be in any fashion deemed liable for any hardship or damages that may befall them after undertaking information described herein.

Additionally, the information in the following pages is intended only for informational purposes and should thus be thought of as universal. As befitting its nature, it is presented without assurance regarding its prolonged validity or interim quality. Trademarks that are mentioned are done without written consent and can in no way be considered an endorsement from the trademark holder.

Table of Contents

Introduction 6

Chapter One: Raspberry Pi 3 7

Chapter Two: Downloading and Installing

    Raspberry Pi.. 13

Chapter Three: Setting Up Raspberry Pi 3 16

Chapter Four: Using Raspberry Pi 3 18

Chapter Five: Raspberry Pi 3 Basics 24

Chapter Six: Installing Windows on a Raspberry

    Pi 3.. 34

Chapter Seven: Raspbian.. 37

Chapter Eight: Using Python with Your Raspberry

    Pi 3.. 40

Chapter Nine: Tips and Tricks to Use with Rasberry

    Pi 3.. 54

Chapter Ten: Creating a Classic Game Emulator 67

Chapter Eleven: Building a Streaming Program for Your Media with a Raspberry Pi 3 Board 73

Chapter Twelve: A Personal Assistant made with Raspberry Pi 3 83

Chapter thirteen: A Wireless Access Point 96

Conclusion 108

Introduction

Congratulations on downloading **Raspberry Pi 3** and thank you for doing so.

The following chapters will discuss everything that you need to know about Raspberry Pi 3. You are not only going to learn what it is and how to install it, but also how to code with it.

There are plenty of books on this subject on the market, thanks again for choosing this one! Every effort was made to ensure it is full of as much useful information as possible, and please enjoy!

Chapter One: Raspberry Pi 3

Raspberry Pi 3 is the latest version of a series of single board computers that was first developed in the United Kingdom by the Raspberry Pi Foundation to promote the basics of computer science in schools as well as countries that are still growing.

When Raspberry Pi was first invented, it became a lot more popular than what the foundation originally anticipated. Because the program sold outside of what the original target market was, the accessories that came with the program were included in several bundles both officially and unofficially.

When asked, the Raspberry Pi foundation will say that over five million of their Pis have been sold before February of 2015 alone, which makes Raspberry Pi the top selling British computer out there. When November of 2016 came around, over eleven million units had been sold.

Raspberry Pi has gone through several generations since the program was first created and released to the public. The very first generation of the program was released in 2012 which was then followed by another model that was inexpensive and straightforward to use. Then two years later, another version came out that had a better design than the previous one. Each of the models is about the size of a credit card and were representing the standard mainline form factor.

With each new design, new capabilities that the previous version did not have before. In January of 2017, the newest model of Raspberry Pi 3 type b was released which typically goes for about thirty-five dollars. However, the new Raspberry Pi zero w was created in February of 2017 which was identical to the Raspberry Pi zero, but with this one, you now have the ability to connect to Wi-Fi and to use Bluetooth.

Each model of the Raspberry Pi comes with a system on a chip that also includes the CPU (central processing unit) as well as the GPU which is the graphics processing unit with a video core iv attached. Most of the CPUs are going to range from 700 MHz to 1.2 GHz with a memory of up to a single GB. The SD cards for the Raspberry devices are going to be inside of the operating system, and they are either going to be the standard size SD card or the micro ones.

Many of the boards that you can buy with Raspberry are going to have up to four slots that you can plug a USB into while also having an HDMI output and video output with a phone jack that you can use for audio.

The foundation makes sure that Raspbian is available for download on any operating system while Python and Scratch are the main programming languages that the Raspberry Pi will use. Because of how it is created, the firmware on the program is going to be closed, but you are going to have the ability to use an open source unofficially.

The concept of Raspberry Pi came around in the early years of 2006, and it is based on the microcontroller Atmel Atmega644. The schematics and layout can be found by anyone in public on the internet.

The trustee of the Raspberry foundation Mr. Eben Upton brought together a unique group of people who were enthusiastic about computers, academics, and several teachers that wanted to try and inspire children through the use of technology.

This machine was inspired by the computer that was created by Acorn in 1981. Each of the model names will indicate which of the models that you are working with based on the British educational Microcomputer that was also developed by Acorn computers. One of the very first prototypes came in a package that was no bigger than a memory stick.

There was a USB port on one end and an HDMI one on the other.

The goal of the foundation was to release two different versions that were between twenty-five and thirty-five dollars. However, orders for a higher priced model began to be accepted in 2012, and the lowest cost model was released in 2015, this model is known as the Raspberry Pi Zero, and it costs around five dollars.

Chapter Two: Downloading and Installing Raspberry Pi

You are not going to be able to run Raspberry Pi without first downloading the operating system.

You can find the software you need at www.RaspberryPi.org.

Noobs

Noobs is a great program for Pi beginners. The word noobs stand for new out of the box software. If you want to, you can download a card that has noobs preinstalled on it from any retailer that sells Pi products. Or, you can go to the Raspberry Pi website and download it from there.

Noobs is easy to use operating system that has Raspbian installed on it in order for you to choose and download an operating system off the internet for your computer.

Noobs Lite is using the same installer but without downloading Raspbian. Everything is thing else is going to be the same.

Raspbian

We are going to go into more detail about Raspbian later on, but this is the official operating system that was created by the foundation and can be installed with NOOB, or you can install it on its own.

Most Raspbian is going to come with the software you need to be preinstalled so that you are able to do more educational programming than you would be able to on NOOBS. Raspbian is also going to come with several different programming languages installed with it.

There is a PIXEL image that lies inside of a ZIP file on the Raspbian operating system where all your features are going to be archived, but the old tools that were used to unzip these files are not going to be supported on all platforms.

In the event that your download for Raspbian is corrupted or is not opening correcting, you are going to want to attempt to use 7Zip or The Unarchiever before trying a reinstall.

Raspberry also supports third-party operating systems such as:

- Ubuntu Mate
- Snappy Ubuntu Core
- Windows 10 IOT Core
- OSMC
- Libreelec
- Pinet
- RISC OS
- And Weather Station

Chapter Three: Setting Up Raspberry Pi 3

Make sure that you have a mouse, keyboard, and a computer monitor or television that you can use for display.

Step one: slide your micro SD card into the SD card slot

Step two: connect you mouse, keyboard, and use an HDMI cord to connect to your display.

Step three: get a power adapter and plug it in.

There should be a red light to indicate that you have completed the setup process. Your operating system will need to be installed after you have set it up and you are going to use noobs for this process. You can install other operating systems if you would like, you do not have to download the ones that are available on the Pi website. However, you are going to have to flush your SD card and start a whole new set up for noobs.

You should notice that there are four raspberries at the top of your boot screen. It is going to show the cores for the processor that will now be set up and running as they should be.

If you want to, you can also light up your LEGS by using a breadboard as well as GPIO ports.

Chapter Four: Using Raspberry Pi 3

When you take a Raspberry board, you are going to be able to set it up and begin programming fairly quickly. You are going to set it up how we discussed previously. The Pi board can be used to create a number of projects, some of which will be talked about later in this book.

You are always going to need a connection to the internet and something to use as a display such as a monitor or television. You are also going to need a mouse, an SD card, and a keyboard.

You are always going be using some sort of code, so it is important to know what commands you will need and what they are going to do and how to use them properly.

There are multiple uses for the Raspberry Pi 3 board. Below are a few things for which you can use the Raspberry Pi board.

Home automation

Many developers are now using Raspberry Pi for home automation. Most of these programmers are taking Raspberry Pi and modifying it so that it is not only energy efficient but cost affordable to those who may not necessarily be able to afford it. The board is going to be able to monitor how much energy is consumed in the household in order to help the family make wiser choices in lowering their bill in the event that they are not able to afford their monthly bill. Thanks to the low cost of the Raspberry Pi board, this is one of the most popular solutions out there because most other solutions are going to be too expensive not only on a commercial level but a private level as well.

Industrial automation

A Polish company by the name of TECHBASE took the Raspberry Pi and became the first to design an industrial computer with it. This equipment is known as ModBerry due to the fact that it runs on the Raspberry Pi compute modules. There are numerous interfaces on this device. There are several serial ports and data can be inputted digitally or manually depending on what the need is. Through this design, Raspberry is no longer just on projects for homes or science, but it is being used to find solutions to a significant number of challenges that industries are facing every day.

Commercial products

The Next Thing Company created an OTTO digital camera that uses the same compute module that is being employed in Poland to automate their industries. Thanks to a kick starter campaign that was started in 2014, the entire project was crowd funded.

There are also other digital tools such as digital media players that use the module for making the device run.

The creators of the Raspberry Pi not only created it for being used on a personal level but for education as well. In 2012, there were questions brought forward to the board located in the United Kingdom in an effort for schools both public and private to get Raspberry Pi in their schools. It was the hope of the school that their school would have more an advantage with the Raspberry Pi in their school.

It was the Premier Farnell CEO that ultimately came forward and said that more schools were interested in the Raspberry Pi and this time it was not just the schools in the United Kingdom, this one was coming from a school that was located in the Middle East. They wanted each girl that was in their school to have a board in order to try and make it easier for these girls to get a job when they graduated school.

In 2014, the foundation decided that it was time to take those that were in their community and hire them so that they could make free learning resources available on their website for those that were wanting access to them. Some of the people that they hired were software developers and ex-teachers who were willing to work together on these resources. Under the creative commons law, the resources are freely licensed so that they are able to be shared with virtually anyone, and the Raspberry foundation encourages sharing these resources with those who need them on social media platforms such as GitHub.

A training course for teachers was also started know as the Picadamy where teachers were assisted in preparing and teaching a more technology-based curriculum through the use of Raspberry Pi in their classroom. It also aided in making sure that the teachers were constantly develoPing professionally through a free course that was run by the education team for the foundation.

It was not until 2017 that an MOOC course was launched working with the University of New South Wales where IoT (internet of things) would use Raspberry Pi online courses.

If you are interested in finding out more about how the Raspberry Foundation is working to further education as technology always changes, then you are free to go on their website and see some of their latest projects!

Chapter Five: Raspberry Pi 3 Basics

Before using Raspberry Pi, you are going to need to know the basics and knowing the basics means that you need to know what the device consists of before you go out and buy one or try and use one. In this section, we are going to learn the hardware and software basics of Raspberry Pi.

Hardware

The hardware for Raspberry Pi has evolved with each version that has come out. These versions have changed how much memory the device has and the peripheral device support.

Processor

Your Broadcom is going to BCM2837 for Raspberry Pi 3 which is going to have a sixty-four-bit quad core with 1.2 GHz. It also contains a 512 KB of shared L2 cache as well as an ARM Cortex A53 processor.

Performance

Raspberry Pi 3 has the quad core processor as we just mentioned which means that it is going to perform ten times faster than the first Raspberry did. This change came around because of the high dependency that there was for tasks that used threading or instruction set use. Most of the benchmarks are going to show you that the third Raspberry is going to be about eighty percent faster than the other Raspberry when it comes to parallelized tasks.

Overclocking

Most of the microprocessors that are used in Raspberry Pi are going to be overclocked at about eight hundred MHz while there are others that have been overclocked at a thousand.

Most of the new versions of Raspberry Pi contain firmware that is going to allow you to choose between about five different presets for overclocking when the device is in use so that you are able to maximize the performance of the SoC without shortening the lifespan of the board itself. The foundation did this by paying close attention to how hot the board became and how long it took for the CPU to load while always changing the clock speeds and the voltage that was put out by the core.

Whenever the CPU demand is weak, or the CPU is running hotter than it should, the performance is going to be slowed down and even stop due to the fact that the CPU is running too hot. When the CPU is running at its optimal temperature, then the chip is going to have an acceptable temperature as well which will in turn increase how fast the performance of the chip is. Depending on the clock speed, it can get up to 1 GHz depending on the board and where the turbo settings are.

Some of the highest presets are going to be around six hundred MHz, but it has been discovered the five hundred MHz can cause corruption to the SD card. Ideally, you are going to want the clock speed to be running somewhere around four hundred and fifty MHz so that you are not damaging the chip and you are not slowing down your CPU.

RAM

The Raspberry Pi 3 is going to run on a single gigabyte of RAM.

Networking

The newest version of Raspberry Pi is going to work with Wi-Fi so that you can connect without the wires. It is also going to have Bluetooth version 4.1 and will use a FullMAC chip that is not going to have any official support when it is in monitor mode. However, it is going to be implemented when you are using an unofficial patch for the firmware that it runs off of. And, if you are not able to get on the internet wirelessly, then you are going to have an ethernet port on the Raspberry 3 that will allow you to connect a ten out of one hundred cables.

Peripherals

All of the Pis are going to be able to have a keyboard and mouse plugged into them. They are not going to require any special equipment when you are using the peripherals. The Pi also has the ability to be used with a mini storage or MIDI converter which means that practically any device or component that has a USB cable on it, you are going to be able to plug into the Raspberry and use.

Video

Most of the video controllers that are on the Raspberry Pi are going to be able to emit what a standard television would emit when it is using HD or full HD as long as the monitor that you are using is able to support it. You can also get a resolution that would be emitted from a CRT TV.

The Pi 3 is not going to come with the proper decoding hardware for H. 265 due to the fact that the CPU is going to be more powerful. But, it is believed that the H. 265 is going to run fast enough that you will be able to decode any videos that may be using H. 265 software.

The graphics processor on the Pi 3 is going to be able to run at a four hundred MHz, therefore, giving you a higher quality of graphics than the previous Pis. The Pis are also going to be able to generate composite video signals as we mentioned earlier in the event that you are using a less expensive monitor with the most standard of connections which will usually be an RCA or a phone connector that is 3.5 millimeters.

Real-time

At the present moment, none of the Pis are going to be able to keep real-time because they are not built with a clock. There is a program that you are going to be able to get however that is going to work around this issue where the Pi is able to get the appropriate time from the network or the server that it is using to boot up which allows the Pi to know what time it is when it is being used.

If you want to provide a consistent time with your Pi for the systems, then you are not going to have to worry because the Pi will automatically save what time it is whenever you go to shut it down, the Pi is simply going to reinstall on the date of the boot.

Accessories

- Camera: back in 2013 the Raspberry Pi Foundation and their distributors were able to release the firmware update that would allow for a camera to be used with the Raspberry Pi. The camera is a flat cable that you are able to plug into the CSI connector. When you are looking at Raspbian, you are going to have to make sure that you enable the camera to run on the board through configuring the camera option. The Raspberry Pi camera is able to take up to a 1080p photo or shoot a 640 x 480p video. Three years later the 8 megaPixels was released to the public.

- Gertboard: the foundation made this accessory for educational purposes only so that the GPIO Pins were able to be expanded so that the interface could be controlled with a series of switches and sensors.
- Infrared camera: this camera was going to be part of the camera module that would not contain the infrared filter, and it is known as the Pi NoIR.

Software

Operating system

As mentioned earlier, you are going to want to try and stick to the Raspbian operating system which is an extension of Linux. There are other operating systems that you are able to use if you do not want to work with a Linux based operating system.

Driver APIs

The video core iv for the graphics processor is going to be using a binary blob which you will be able to prime into the graphics processing unit from an SD card and then only adding in the additional software when it has booted up. Most of the work that is done with the driver is going to be done with a closed source for the graphics processor and its related code. Any software use calls are going to run their code closed source, but there are specific applications that you can download in order to open the driver of origin that is inside of the kernel. The kernel's API is going to be designed for these closed libraries in order to make sure that it the Pi is processing correctly, and the code is not being messed with which could end up causing the Pi not to operate properly.

Firmware

All of the firmware that the Raspberry Pi uses is going to be closed sourced and use a binary blob that is freely redistributable. You are not going to find a lot of firmware that is going to be open source for the Pi.

Chapter Six: Installing Windows on a Raspberry Pi 3

Windows 10 released the operating system that would work on multiple single board computers. This opened it up to where it would work with Raspbian. But you can also put Windows 10 on your Pi board.

Step one: create an account with Microsoft connect

Step two: find the download for windows_iot_coreRPI3_build.zip file. This file is going to contain a file titled flash.ffu. This data needs to be kept in a place that you can access it later.

Step three: take a 8 GB Class 10 SD card and place it on your computer.

Step four: Open up your command prompt and enter this code:

Syntax

Diskpart

List disk

Exit

You will be able to locate the number for the drive that your SD card is connected to.

Step five: Microsoft has a set of instructions that you will need to follow in order to flash your SD card in Windows 10.

There is an administrator command prompt that you will use in order to place the image on your SD card by running this prompt. You are going to replace physical drive n with the drive number.

Syntax

Dism.exe / apply – image / imagefile : flash. Ffu

\ applydrive: \\ . \ physicaldriven / skipplatformcheck

Step six:

Take the SD card out and place it on your Pi board because Windows 10 is ready to boot up on your board.

Chapter Seven: Raspbian

Raspbian was created by the Raspberry Pi foundation as a Debian computer operating system that was to be used with Raspberry Pi. Mike Thompson and Peter Green were the ones who created Raspbian as a side project while they were working with the foundation. At first, the operating system was completed in June of 2012, but it is still constantly under active development so that the operating system can be changed and produce better results with each new version that is released. Raspbian is optimized so that it will work even with the CPUs that have a low performance.

Just like any other operating system, Raspbian is going to use a desktop environment known as PIXEL. PIXEL stands for Pi Improved Xwindows Environment Lightweight. Not only does it work on a desktop, but it is going to be able to be modified in order to work with an LXDE environment and can be stacked with the window manager known as Openbox so that an entirely new theme emerges.

Raspbian is sent out with a copy of the Mathematica program as well as the Raspberry version of Minecraft and Chromium. But, with Chromium, it is going to be a lightweight version so that it is able to be used with the Raspberry Pi system.

When you look at Raspbian it is going to do more than give you an operating system that is pure; it is also going to come with thirty-five thousand software bundles that are preinstalled and already formatted so that they can be installed onto your Pi without giving you any issue.

These preinstalled packages are meant to give you the best performance possible for your Pi, and they are always being updated so that you are constantly given the best optimization for your operating system.

The newest version of Raspbian was released March of 2017 and is version 4.4. This is an updated version of Debian Jessie.

Chapter Eight: Using Python with Your Raspberry Pi 3

Before you can get started using Python with Raspberry Pi you are going to need to gather some supplies in order to complete all of the steps that are required to do what you need to do with python.

- A micro USB cable
- A Raspberry board
- An Ethernet cable (this is going to give you a faster download speed than if you were to use the wi-fi)
- A microSD card that is 4 GB or bigger. You are going to want to try and stick to a class 10 card or better.
- A resin.io account
- A micro power supply that is 2A and uses a USB cord

You have to know how to use python with your board before you are able to build anything with your board. In the event that you are using resin.io and you are unsure of what to do next, there is a team of people who are going to be there to help you

Here are some of the moving parts of resin.io:

- Application: this is the devices that are going to run the same application code. Whenever a device is provisioned, it is going to be associated with the application. There is no limit to how many devices can be on the application. You also have the option of moving devices to different applications.
- Resin remote: this is the repository that is going to be tied to your application.when a code is pushed onto the master branch, a repo is going to be built and then deployed as a container to any device that is tied to

that application. SSH keys are going to be used to secure it, therefore, do not forget to set up the SSH key.
- Container: this container is used with docker.
-

SSH key

The SSH key is going to be used in securing the connection whenever code is sent to a program. To ensure the git connection, you are going to need to add the public SSH key. The private SSH key should never be shared with anyone.

All you are going to do is paste the public key into the UI box and make sure that you hit save. Or, you can import the key from Github.

Should you not have an SSH key, you should look at the documents provided by Github on how to generate the key pair for the operating system that you are working on.

After you have created the SSH key, it is going to be easy to use. You are not going to have to think about it at all. After you have set up the git push in your code, resin.io is going to take care of everything else.

You can also import the SSH key from Github by clicking on the Octocat icon. You are then going to be prompted to enter your username into the prompt that appears on your screen. you are going to need to set up and save your SSH key that you have imported before you go on to the next step.

Creating applications

In order to create a request, you are going to type the name at the prompt and choose which Raspberry Pi model it is from the menu before you hit the create button. You are going to now be taken to a new dashboard that is going to be specific to that application.

The dashboard is going to change as you continue to command and manage your fleet with Raspberry Pi 3.

Adding a device

On your dashboard, there is going to be a section that informs you of every device that is connected to your application. Not only that, but it is going to show their logs and their status.

You are going to need to click on the download resinOS in order to get that operating system. From here a list of versions that are available will be in your dropdown. The most recent version is going to be the one that you are going to want to use.

Warning: the versions that have the suffix .dev will be used for development purposes only which mean that they should not be used while in production.

Note: your .img is going to appear to be larger than it was before. However, your browser is going to download a compressed version of that photo and then decompress it so that the download goes by faster.

Before the downloading of this image starts, you are going to be asked how your device is currently hooked up to the internet that you are using. There are going to be two options that you are going to be able to choose from.

- Wifi: if you choose this option you are going to need to specify what your networks name is as well as a passphrase for the network that your device is connected to.
- Ethernet cable: there is not going to be any configuration for you if you use this as the default option.

After you have Picked how your device is connected, you are going to select the download device OS button so that you get the image for the resin.io operating system in order to configure it to your network as well as your application.

Once the download has finished, you are going to have a file with the suffix of .img and a name that is long with a bunch of numbers. There is a bit of text that says myfleet which is going to be the name of the application that you created.

Deploying code

After getting some of your devices connected, you are going to be able to implement the code so that you can start to use it to build your projects.

TyPically, the first project that you are going to do is a web server using flask which is going to serve as a static page.

You are going to need to put your code into your preferred git client. The repo is going to clone the project before changing the directory into a new directory and adding the resin git remote endpoint by running the command "get remote add" in the right-hand corner of your application page.

Note: on any other git client, you are going to have a different way to add the repository.

Since you now have your reference set up, you are going to add it to the application's remote repository. That way when you push any new changes, it is going to be comPiled and built into the server before being deployed to every device that is in that application's fleet.

So that you can deploy the code to all of your devices you are going to run this code:

$ git push resin master

In the event that you have to or want to replace the source code for your application with something new, you are going to need to force your push by running the code:

Git push resin master - - force

Note: when you perform your first push, git is going to ask if you want to add this to your list of allowed hosts, enter the word yes and continue with your coding.

Your code will be successfully comPiled and built whenever the unicorn appears in the terminal. This is going to mean that it has been saved to the program's image registry. The estimated time that this is going to take is about two minutes; any builds after this are going to be quicker due to build catching.

Now your application can be downloaded and carried out on all the devices connected to your application. You may have to wait up to six minutes for the first push to be completed. Your pushes that are done after this are going to go faster.

At this point in time, you will have a python web server that is running on the device and the logs are going to be seen on your dashboard. You can enable a public URL by going to the Actions page on the device settings from your dashboard. This URL is going to be able to be accessed anywhere in the world.

With Python being a coding program, there is not going to be much that you are not able to do. If you can code it with Python, then the chances are that you are going to be able to code it and use Raspberry Pi with it. You are just going to have to keep in mind that the Pi board is not going to do everything and you are going ot have to ensure that the prorams you are coding are going to go through the Pi program without any problem.

Desktop sense hat emulator

The sense hat emulator was designed to runo n the Raspberry Pi desktop rather than using a browser.

There are going to be sliders that you can use in order to change the values of your sensors.

You are going to want two versions so that you can

- Integrate the sense hat program with any Python module that is available or even with other Pi features like the camera module.
- To use it offline
- To accommodate the 256 MB modles of Pi that are not able to run the web version.

Your emulator is going to come pre installed on the Raspbian release however, you can also install it by using the terminal and entering this code.

Sudo apt- get update

Sudo apt- get install python – sense- emu python3 – sense – emu

Python- sense- emu- doc sense -emu-tools -y

Fromt here you are going to be able to access the emmulator from the desktop under the programming title.

This emulator is going to simulate the sense hat hardware that is attached to pi. You will be able to read the sensors or write the LED matrix that will be used in running multiple Python processes.

Your code needs to be written in IDLE like you have done before. In the event that you are wanting to port your code into a physical sense hat then you are going to need to change a bit of the coding.

This code

Sense_emu

Needs to be changed to

Sense_hat

At the very top of your program you are going to be able to reverse the porting to the emulator. But, this step is not going to be required in the web version of the emulator.

The emulator has a various number of preferences that are going to enable you to adjust the behavior of the emulator such as the sensor simulation that is also known as jitter. This is going to cost some of the time tha tis on the CPU and is also going to turn off the low end Raspberry Pis, however it will provide a realistic experience of the hardware sensors and how they are going to behave. You are going to behave. You are going to see the values that are being returned to you in your code according to the tolerance for errors of the physical sensors tha tyou are using on the sense hat.

The emulator is also going to allow the users of Raspberry Pi to participate in the Astro Pi competitions without the need to buy a sense hat which is ideal for the classroom when the sense hat may be beyond the school's current budget.

In case you are new to sense hat, you will copy and past a lot of the code that you see in the eduactional examples or you can look at other resources that are going to show you how to use the sense hat emulator.

The emulator can be installed on a Linux desktop such as Ubuntu if you are using that desktop.

Sense hat egg drop

There is a game from sense hat and Raspberry Pi that was created by a UK teacher where you can build the game and not only learn coding, but also learn science as well. In this game you are going be using the sensors for motion and humidity to determine how long it will take the egg to reach the ground and where it is going to land.

This is typically a science experiment that is done with high school kids to learn about mass and velocity. With Python and Raspberry Pi you are going to be able to do this but without the mess. On top of that, you are going to be able to look at other factors that are going to determine where the egg will land and how long it will take to reach the ground.

Chapter Nine: Tips and Tricks to Use with Rasberry Pi 3

Have you ever noticed that when you have some suggestions and tricks to use with the program that you are using, it makes it a lot easier to use that program? There are not too many things for which you cannot find tips and tricks to simplify use, and Raspberry Pi is no exception. Being that Raspberry is just like everything else, we are going to explore some of the tips and tricks that you can practice with Raspberry Pi in order to make it more enjoyable and easier for you to use.

Changing Your Keyboard Layout

When you first start using Raspbian, the keyboard that is automatically recognized is the Great Britain character set. However, if you want to change how your keyboard looks to something that may be more familiar to you such as the US keyboard, then you are going to have to get into the file that holds the configuration for the keyboard and edit it.

The first command that you need to execute is this one:

Sudo nano/ etc/ default/ keyboard

This is where your keyboard file is going to open up and will hold all of the code that has your keyboard set to the GB default setting. You are going to have to change the keyboard to the US keyboard that you want to use. You are going to see that your xblayout says GB and what you are going to do is go to this input and delete GB and input US.

There is no need for you to change anything else! All you are going to have to do is reboot your Pi so that the changes take effect and you have successfully changed your keyboard!

Changing the Default Local Time

It is always irritating when you are working on something that does not say the time that is right for where you are located. Raspbian is set to give you the UTC time zone automatically; however, you are going to be able to adjust it so that it represents your time zone instead.

First, enter the command
Sudo dpkg – reconfigure tzdata

Once this command has been executed, you are going to be able to Pick which time zone that you are residing in. After you have completed this action, you are going to reboot Raspberry Pi.

Whenever Raspberry Pi starts back up, you can use the command date to check the date and time to ensure that it is in the proper time zone. You should get the result of the day, the month, the date, the time, your time zone, and the year as your outcome.

Accessing your Pi with the name or the IP address

There are not very many people who know how to access a web page by using the IP address of the server that they are currently connected to. But, you are going to be able to as long as you add in the hostname of the computer that you are using to use Pi. In doing this, you are going to be able to use the name of the Pi device rather than the IP address.

Now, for this example, you are going to be accessing your Pi from a machine that is running off of Windows 7. There are obviously going to be subtle changes that you are going to have to change in order to make it work on a different operating system.

Make sure that you have administrative permissions on the computer that you are using or else you are not going to have the ability to edit the files that need to be modified.

First, you are going to browse your system for the driver's directory. This will be your host file, and it should have all of the drivers that your computer uses to run. What you will need to do is include the IP address for you Pi and the name that you assigned to it.

Whenever your local domain is reserved for SUDN (exclusive use domain name), then you are going to be seeing the domain name that has been utilized for the network usage inside of your machine. You are not going to be capable of configuring this like you will be able to set up the FQDN (fully qualified domain name), so your local names need to ensure that they are not conflicting with any external addresses that are located on your system.

So, at the bottom of your file, you should have the local host IP address as well as the IP address for your Pi. You should be able to type http://Pi.local into the browser now that you use and see the web page that is set up to be displayed on your Pi device automatically.

With the Linux system, your host file is going to be located in the /, etc. directory, and for those that are using Apple, you may need to go to the Bonjour service to find the host file that you need to edit.

Transferring files to and from your Pi

Whenever you are working with simple files on your Raspberry Pi, then you are going to have the ability to copy the code so that you can transfer the file to your Pi. Some people are going to say that it is not going to be easy to take this code and move it from the archive that you are working on to a different machine, but with the use of GUI, you are going to be able to accomplish your task without too much trouble.

You need to make sure that you are familiar with SSH file transfers or SFTP, you also need to have them on your computer where you can access them so that you can get the task down. SSH is going to be the secure shell. You can use an FTP without using an SSH but if that is the case you might as well just use the SFTP to ensure that everything stays secure.

The program FileZilla is going to be used to complete your transfer, and you are going to go to the FileZilla website in order to download it to your computer so that it can be used. This application is free of charge and opens sourced to ensure that you have access to all of the options that you are needing or wanting.

After the download is complete, there is going to be the proper software on your desktop; you should also download a zipped software, but try and avoid the installer due to the fact that the installer is going to give you software that you are not going to use necessarily.

Okay, now that you have everything installed, you are going to be on the main interface of the program. From here you are going to select the file that you want to transfer as well as the site manager that is located on the main menu so that a connection is established between the two computers.

A dialogue box should pop up that enables you to enter all of the details for the connection for your Raspberry Pi. You will need to click on the button that says "new site" and enter in all of the information below.

- The host box needs to have the IP address that is assigned to your Raspberry Pi board.
- The protocol needs to be changed to the SFTP SSH protocol.
- The logon type should be set to normal.
- Your login name needs to be entered into the user box
- Your password will then need to be placed into the password box.
- In the event that you want to rename your connection, you are going to be able to. This is recommended if you are working with multiple connections at once or to several different Raspberry Pi boards.

After you have completed this step, you will click on connect so that the connection is established. If this is the first time that you are doing this, then you are going to receive a warning box that is going to want to make sure that you are wanting to keep doing what it is that you are doing. Being that you are the host, you will want to click ok to continue with your process. If you are going to use this host for more connections in the future, then you will need to click the box that says you trust the host so that you do not have to approve of the host again in the future.

Your GUI is going to now be on your desktop, and the files for the Pi will be on the right side of the window. This is where you are going to have the capabilities to drag and drop files between your two computers so that you have access to what you need on the proper computer.

Editing files on the Pi with a desktop editor

Now that you can see the files that are on your Pi with the FileZilla program, you are going to go a step further and edit them on your desktop with your editor of choice. What you will do is log into the remote desktop session with your Pi and the desktop that is connected to it.

The first thing you are going to do is find a file in your Pi window that you want to edit and right click on that file. Here is where you will need to select the view and edit option. Should the file not have any program associated with it that will allow it to be modified, you are going to be able to find one on your desktop that you like to work with before hitting the okay button.

From there the file is going to be opened in your editor so that you can work on it until it is exactly how you want it to be. At the point that you have completed editing the file, ensure that you save it. Another dialog box is going to appear, and you will be asked if you want to update the file back to your Pi server. Make sure that you click on yes! This is done to make sure that you can edit the file and keep a local file on your desktop. Essentially, you are creating a backup file on both machines in the event that you need to edit the file again.

Turning the activity light on and off

Your Raspberry Pi board is going to have LEDs that tell you whenever you have power going through it and whenever the SD card is being accessed. You can find these lights at the end near your GPIO Pins. The first thing you need to do is execute this command. However, you cannot just use the sudo command; you are going to have to switch the root user as well.

Sudo -i

The I option is going to gather the root user's environment to ensure you are working on the right board in the event that you run multiple boards.

Your code is now going to show you which root user you are connected to so that you know that you are on the proper board. It is at this time that you are going to be able to turn the LED on or off by using a particular set of code.

To turn the LED on you will use this code:

Echo 1 >/ sys/ class/ leds/ led0/ brightness

To turn the LED off

Echo mmc0 > / sys/ class/ leds/ led0/ brightness

Once you have turned the LED on or off, you need to log out of the root user by click on exit or using the Ctrl plus d button.

Your /sys directory is going to work on the interface that is located between the user space and the kernel space. Since this is an implementation system file, the subdirectory is going to be pulled out of the kernel during runtime so that the devices that are running on the system are presented as a class.

You are going to see a highly complex hierarchy in your directory that is going to give you all of the classes and the links to those categories.

The class for your LEDs is going to be led0 or led1. While looking in the directory, you are going to have to find the trigger file so that you can see where the modules are in the kernel and which activity is going to be used to show the brightness of the LED.

Your LED is only going to work on two different levels of brightness, so essentially you are only able to turn the LED on and off which is going to be represented by a one or a zero. One is going to turn the LED on, and zero is going to turn the LED off.

Chapter Ten: Creating a Classic Game Emulator

With the Raspberry Pi 3 board, you are going to be working with a board that has incredible speed and is going to be different to work with than the Raspberry boards that came before it.

One of the things that the board offers you is the choice to turn it into a game emulator that is going to offer you the option to play some of your favorite classic games. And, who does not like to play the classics from time to time especially when you are trying to show your kids where their advanced video games came from?

Please note that unless you own a physical copy of the game, you are going to be creating a ROM illegally. Therefore, you are going to want to stick to the games that you own a physical copy of so that you are not putting yourself at risk of being caught and punished by the federal government. This can mean that you are fined or even sent to prison for having an illegal copy of the game.

Before you can begin, you are going to need to gather your equipment. Here is a list of the things that you are going to need to have in order to create your game emulator.

- A game controller with USB connectors
- A Raspberry Pi 3 Model B board
- The proper cables that will allow you to hook your board into the HDMI ports on the TV or monitor that you are going to be playing on.
- A case for your Raspberry board
- Keyboard and mouse that offers you a USB connection
- Micro SD card
- The HDMI cable that you are going to hook into your display device
- A power supply for the board

1. The primary thing that you are going to do is download the retro Pie project onto the hard drive of your computer. You will be able to obtain the download file on the retro Pie website.
2. At this point, you will need to download another image by the name of Win32DiskImager. After this has been downloaded, you will take the retro Pie file that is on your hard drive and move it to the SD card that you gathered when you were getting all of your equipment together. Before you write the image onto the SD card, you should ensure that you have the details correct so that you are not writing the image somewhere that it does not need to be.
3. Once you have the image printed onto the SD card, you will remove that SD card from your computer and put it into your Pi board. From here, you are also going to connect everything to the appropriate ports so that you do not have to do it later on.

4. Your PI should automatically boot up the retro Pie. After it has booted up, you are going to need to press F4 so that you get the command prompt opened on your screen.
5. After the command prompt has opened, you will enter the code: sudo rasPi config
6. The expanded file system needs to be selected before you hit accept.
7. Now back to your main screen, you will go to options and locate the SSH option under the advanced options. If it is not already authorized, you will need to enable it.
8. Moving on to overclock, you will choose medium unless you are playing games that have graphics that are more complex, in this case, you are going to Pick the higher option.
9. Just like always, you will finish with your options and then reboot your board.
10. After the restart is done, you are going to go to the main screen which is now going to be able to load your game emulators.

11. Your Pi board needs to be connected to your home network, and after you have ensured that it is connected, you will need to go to your network that is located in the windows explorer. There should be a table of devices that are attached to the network, and you will need to go to the one that is labeled RaspberryPi. You will need to double click it.
12. There is going to be a folder titled ROMS, and this is going to be the folder where all of your games are going to be stored as they pertain to the game emulator.
13. Your ROMS have to be unzipped before you are able to load them where they need to be loaded.

Please remember that if you do not have access to your Raspberry Pi because of the connection that it has to your internet, you can try one of these solutions.

- Take an empty USB drive and plug it into your Raspberry Pi 3 board.
- Wait until the light quits flashing before you pull the USB out of the port on your board and plug it into your machine.
- There should be an empty directory on the USB that is constructed just for the ROM files that you want to play.
- The ROM files that you have unzipped will need to be coPied and placed into their appropriate directories on your USB drive.
- Unplug the USB from your computer and plug it back into your Raspberry Pi.
- Once again, wait for the activity light to stop blinking so that you know all of the files have been reproduced over on your Raspberry Pi.

Congratulations! You can now play your classic games with your Raspberry Pi 3!

Chapter Eleven: Building a Streaming Program for Your Media with a Raspberry Pi 3 Board

This is going to be helpful when you find yourself owning an extensive collection of movies, music, and television shows that you have bought over the years. However, because you have so much, you most likely have forgotten what you own, and it is "collecting dust" on your hard drive.

You can set up a streaming program that is similar to Netflix and Pandora by using the Plex Media Server software that you are able to get for free!

To do this, you will be required to collect these Pieces of equipment:

- Your laptop your desktop depending on which one you want to work off of.
- Your Raspberry Pi 3 board

- A micro SD card
- A hard drive that is going to have enough power to support the streaming program that you are creating.
- A power supply for your Pi board. It is recommended that you use a 5V 2A power supply.
- HDMI cable to connect your Pi board to your laptop or desktop.
- A keyboard and mouse for the setup.
- You may also want to look into getting a heat sink for your chips due to the fact that using your board for multimedia consumption is going to cause them to get hot and potentially melt.
- An ethernet cable to access your home network if you are not working off of Wi-Fi.

1. To start, you are going to install the NOOBS operating system off of the foundation's website. You will need to go through an unzipPing process that is going to extract the files that you are going to need.
2. Place your SD card into your PC and format it so that it is using the Gnome Disk Utility.
3. Now you are going to need to change the directory that is on your SD card. You are going to do this by inserting this code into the command prompt. Cd / path_ of_ USB.
4. The NOOBS file needs to be unzipped on your SD card; this can be done by using this code: unzip PATH _ OF_ NOOBS
5. It is crucial that you make sure that the contents that are in your NOOBS folder are transferred to the root directory that is on your SD card.
6. At this point in time, you are going to need to plug your mouse, keyboard, and monitor into your Pi board while putting your SD card into the board as well. It is not a bad

idea for you to also connect the power supply to the board as well.

7. Your system should automatically start NOOBS so that you are able to install the operating system that you want to use. You will most likely want to install Raspbian.

8. After the installation is completed, you are going to need to reboot your Raspbian board so that it is now running on the new operating system. All of the files on your system are going to automatically be resized so that they are using the space that is open on the SD card.

9. Using your ethernet cable is going to give you the fastest speed during installation processes; however, you do not have to use it if you do not want to. But, you are going to need to get online with your new operating system and open the command prompt.

10. Enter this code at your command prompt so that you are able to find the IP address that is associated with your Raspberry Pi board. If config

11. After getting your IP address, you will reopen your terminal that is located on your laptop and change the SSH that is on your Pi.
12. By default the password for your Raspberry Pi board is going to be Raspberry; however, you can always change this if you want to.
13. Here is where you are going to need to update your system before your next install. It is always best for you to practice with a new distro when it comes to any software installations.
14. After you have updated your board, you will take the external hard drive and plug it into your Pi via one of the USB ports. Your hard drive needs to be formatted to ext4 in order to give you the best compatibility with the Linux system.
15. Now mount your hard drive and make an entry in the fstab so that the hard drive automatically mounts each time that you have to reboot.

16. At this point in time, you are going to install the Plex Media Server. Being that you are using a package that was created by a third party, you need to have their GPG key. For Plex Media, the GPG key is going to be: wget – o – https:// dev2day. De/ pms/ dev2day-pms. Gpg. Key sudo apt- key- add

17. Your repos also need to be included in the source file. Echo "deb https://dev2day. De/ pms/ jessie main" sudo tee / etc/ apt/ sources. List. d/ pms. List

18. Update your system again so that you are running off of the latest data that is available.

19. Plex Media Server can now be installed with this code. Sudo apt- get install – t jessie plexmediaserver – y

20. After it has installed, you are going to be able to run the service with this code: service plexmediaserver star

That is just the first part of building your own streaming program. At this point in time, you are going to now begin to set up your media server so that you can move your multimedia over to the Raspberry Pi board so that you can stream it without having it sit on your computer taking up space that you could be using for something else.

1. Setting Plex Media up is going to be a simple process, all you are going to be required to do is obey the instructions that appear on your screen. After it has been set up, you will be able to direct the service towards where your media files are in order to move them over. This can be done on any laptop or desktop that is working off of your network. All you are going to need to do is type the IP address of your Pi board into the web browser.

2. By transcribing the IP address into the browser, you are going to be opening the interface for Plex Media. Plex has a great feature that allows for it to gather information that is located on the internet

and taking your media files. But, you need to make sure that you have your media categorized appropriately or else Plex is not going to know that it is a file that it needs to grab. Therefore, you will want to create folders on your hard drive and place all of your multimedia in them. You may want to make folders with names such as "TV shows," "photos," "family videos," etc. Should you move a file into a folder where it does not belong, then Plex is not going to recognize them, and you are not going to be able to stream them.

3. Now, open the movie tab on your Plex interface and look at the folders that you are going to be allowed to browse. You should select the proper file that is on your hard drive so that they are moved into the new program. Do not rush the program because it is going to need time to scan and process all of the files that you put into it.

4. Not only are you going to be able to access your own multimedia files, but you will also be able to locate video channels online. To do this, you are going to go to the channels tab and install the channels that you are going to watch with Plex.

Awesome! You have now put all of your multimedia on Plex! But, how do you access Plex so that you can play that multimedia?

1. Open your browser on the network that you first started working with Plex on and put the IP number of your Raspberry Pi into the URL ribbon.
2. This is going to cause Plex to open automatically. All you are going to need to do is log into the media service and select what it is that you want to watch. Plex also can be modified from the interface that appears on your screen.
3. Before anything appears on your screen, you are going to be asked to set up the Plex

Media Player before plugging in the HDMI cable so that your Raspberry Pi is being displayed here you can see it.
4. To access the contents of Plex on a different network, you have the option of purchasing a PlexPass which will then enable you to stream the content of your Plex account on any apparatus that is connected to the internet. With this, you are also going to be able to share your Plex with your family members.

And there you have it! You have now created your own streaming program!

Chapter Twelve: A Personal Assistant made with Raspberry Pi 3

Personal assistants are going to come in handy when you are working on multiple projects and need an extra "brain" to help you remember what it is that you are supposed to be doing. The computer that is being coded to be your personal assistant is going to be smarter in some ways than a person is because a computer has more technology at its "fingertips" then a person may. Not to mention, you can talk to your pc and get the information you need without ever having to stop what you were doing.

In order to complete this project, you will need:

- A mouse and keyboard that will attach to your Raspberry Pi 3 board via a USB connector.
- An HDMI cable and a television that supports HDMI.
- A Raspberry Pi 3 board that already has Raspbian Wheezy installed on it.
- Extra wires.
- A Wi-Fi adapter with a USB connection.
- A double pole double is thrown relays that run off of five volts.
- A USB soundcard
- Part of a vero board
- A five-volt power supply
- A five-volt amplifier, you are going to want to keep this small so that it can be held close to your Pi board.

1. Update your Raspberry Pi board; you will need to connect your board to your network via an ethernet cable so that you are getting faster speeds than if you were just working off of a Wi-Fi connection.
2. After you have updated your board, you will need to shut it down so that the new updates are applied.
3. Before using the power back on to your board, you are going to need to connect your Wi-Fi adaptor.
4. Once booted up, go to the desktop and select the option that is going to allow you to configure your Wi-Fi settings. From here a new window is going to be opened.
5. Select the scan button so that another new window is opened.
6. In this window, you will go to the SSID and double click it.
7. A third window is going to be opened, and you are going to need to enter your password into the PSK box before clicking add.

8. Moving back to the first window that opened, you will be able to check the IP address and see that you are connected to your wireless network.
9. Shut your Pi board down once more.

After you have done that, you will be ready to set up the hardware that is associated with creating your personal assistant.

1. Open the plastic case for your sound card; you are going to desolder some of the connectors. You will need to solder where the connectors are so you are not harming the actual sound card components.
2. Taking your DPDT relais, you are going to make the push button on the intercom that you have gotten and connect the DPDT to that button. The second wire that is attached to the switch will need to go into the relay coil while the first wire goes to the ground. This way whenever the button is pushed, you are activating the coil and relay

switches. You can also add a diode in the opposite direction over your two Pins that are connected to the coil.
3. The Pins that are in the middle of your DPDT relays are going to have a positive and negative connection that is going to go to your speaker. The Pins that are usually open are going to be attached to the microphone's input for the soundcard. The Pins that are normally closed will be the output of the soundcard. However, you may find that the signal for your output is not going to be loud enough, this is why you need to have your amplifier.
4. Take the five-volt Pin for your amplifier and the five volt GND Pin and connect them so that you now have power flowing through your amplifier from the soundcard. You will need to connect the R+ to the R- to the Pins that are typically closed in your relay.
5. After you have done this, put everything into the intercom case and then connect your sound card to your Raspberry Pi board.

6. It is not recommended that you try to power everything from your board, that is why you may want to consider getting a three amp wall adapter. Depending on the wall adaptor that you get will depend on if you have to cut the connector to the adaptor and connect a USB connector so that you can power your board.
7. After you have cooked everything up, you will need to close the case for your intercom.
8. Take your sound card and configure it by opening your configuration file. You can do this by putting this code into your command prompt. Sudo nano/ etc/ mod probe. d/alsa- base . conf.
9. The part of your code that says: options snd- USB- audio index = -2 to where it says the same thing except your index is going to be 0.
10. Reboot your Pi board so that the new changes can be applied.

You are now at the point that you are going to be setting up the software that you need to run your voice commands.

1. It is recommended that you use the Steven Hickson voice command software that is going to allow you to have an easy setup and simple to use interface all while being reliable for whatever it is that you are using it for. The software can be located on his website and downloaded for you to use.
2. After you have installed the appropriate voice software, you will input this command. Voice command -s
3. It is with this command that you are going to be able to use the setup wizard and go through it to set up the voice command that is appropriate for your device.
4. After set up you need to enter the voice command -e so that your configure file will open and enable you to set up the commando's that you need and the actions that are related to it.

5. For configuration you will need to enter the script command = = action it is with this command that you are going to be able to set up the commands that you want your personal assistant to do. So, if you say play, then the program is going to know that you want it to play music. But, if you say something such as play game it will open up your chess game. You will be able to put in any command that you wish to be executed by your personal assistant.
6. After you have completed the editing process for your configuration file, you need to save it. Upon saving, everything is going to be ready for you to use.
7. In order to run the voice command software, you will enter the code voice command-c.

Your personal assistant is now ready to be used! Your personal assistant is going to be able to list to the commands that you give it and execute them appropriately. In the case that your command cannot be executed, then your personal assistant is going to take to the internet and find the answer that you are looking for. DesPite the fact that your personal assistant can now execute your voice commands, you are not quite done.

1. You are going to make it to where your voice command starts whenever you launch the program. In order to do this, you are going to go to your Raspberry Pi home directory and select the configuration directory.
2. Once in this directory, you are going to create a new list.
3. After it is created, you will need to access this directory.
4. A new file has to be created in the directory with this script. Sudo nano voice command. Desktop
5. Open the file you created and insert the code that is going to cause your voice command to start up whenever you execute the program.

[entry for desktop]

Type = application

Name = voicecommand

Exec = voice command – c

Startupnotify = false

6. Ensure your file has been saved before you reboot your Raspberry Pi 3, board.

Your personal assistant is going to be able to open up programs and gather information from the internet, however, there are going to be times that you want a specific type of information to be returned to you in a particular way. In order to do this, you are going to write out your own script using Python so that you can get this data from the internet and the data that you do not want is not going to even make its way to you due to the fact that it is not what you are looking for.

The biggest issue for this though is that your script is going to be written out and executed as text rather than speech, but there is going to be a script that is going to enable you to have your personal assistant talk to you.

1. The first step that you are going to need to go through is to get a text2speech.sh script. You can find this script online, or you can go to the blog of Oscar Liang and get his script that he has written out to convert text to speech.
2. The script that you choose is going to need to be put into your nano or text editor on your graphics desktop.
3. Just like any Piece of code that you put into your Raspberry Pi, you need to ensure that your script is saved and then made so that it is executable. You can do this with the following code.

Chmod +x text2speech .sh

4. By preparing this, you are going to be making the code usable for any applications that have the capability to convert text into speech.
5. The next step is to create the Python script that is going to work with the text to speech script that we have put into our program. For every script that you use, you are going to need to have a similar Python script. Your code is going to look something like this.

#!/ bin/ bash

Result = $(python the name of the python script you are using. Py)

./ text2speech. Sh $result

6. This script needs to be saved under any name that you want it to be saved under and then made executable as every bit of code needs to be made.

7. At this point in time, the code that you have written out can now go to your configuration file that you have for your voice command and then any text that is researched by your "personal assistant" is going to be spoken to you in the event that you have inserted the appropriate command.

That is it! Your personal assistant is complete and ready for you to use it.

Chapter thirteen: A Wireless Access Point

What you need

- Your Raspberry Pi
- An ethernet cable that will connect to the network you are using
- An SD boot card for you Raspberry Pi
- A device that is going to support access point and has a USB Wi-Fi port

How it will work

As mentioned earlier, you are going to be able to create a Wi-Fi Hotspot for those devices that need to have access to the internet but cannot plug directly into the internet; it is going to work much like an internet café does.

In simplified terms, you are going to be:

- Creating an access point to the Wi-Fi and broadcasting it on the channel of your choosing.
- Assigning an IP address to the devices that are going to use your access point to connect to the network.
- Joining the wireless and the wired networks together through the use of a Network Address Translation.

Step one:

1. Make sure that you possess all of the appropriate software installed. You are going to be able to find the software that you need online. You may find that it looks something similar to this.

Sudo aptitude install hostapd hostap- utils iw bridge- utils

2. Go into the file and edit the Hostapd part of the file. You are going to see something like this: sudo nano/ etc/ init.d/ hostapd

You are going to need to attach the DAEMON line so that you are able to create your access point. Your code for the DAEMON line will be this: DAEMON_ CONF = / etc/ hostapd/ hostapd. Conf

Now you are going to need to make sure you save your file and exit it so that you are not making any unnecessary changes.

3. This is the point where you are going to need to configure the hostapd.cof. you will be creating an open network or a WPA network that is secured. It is highly recommended that you create a secure network in order to make sure that no one is getting ahold of your access point and tampering with it thus allowing hackers to get into your devices and gather information that they should not have access to.

In order to do this, you are going to need to edit your file for the hostapd.cof so that the network that you create is secure. If this file is not automatically created when you download the software that you need, then you are going to need to create this file and ensure that you are adding these lines of code.

Sudo nano / etc/ hostapd/ hostapd.cof

Ctrl_ interface = / var/ run/ hostapd

This is going to be the basic configuration for your access point.

Macaddr _ acl = 0 autho_ algs =1

Many of your more up to date wireless drivers are going to have the kernel driver.

For your local configuration, you will use this code

Interface = wlan0

Bridge = br0

Hw_mode = g

Ieee80211n=1

Channel = 1

Ssid = raspberry pi _ ap

Macaddr_ acl = 0

Autho_algs = 1

Ignore _ broadcast _ ssid = 0

Wpa = 3

Wpa _ passphrase = MY_ PASSPHRASE
Wpa_ key_ mgmt. = WPA- PSK

Wpa_ pairwise = TKIP

Rsn _ pairwise = CCMP

Ensure that you are saving and closing your file when you are done adding in the code that needs to be added!

It is also essential to know that you need to change the ssid, the channel, and the passphrase to things that only you are going to know and the people who are accessing your internet will know. The ssid is typically going to be the name of the hotspot that you have created that other devices are going to see. The passphrase is going to be the password that you are using to ensure that your network is secure from hackers and those that would want to get into your internet and gather your personal information.

Chapter fourteen: Command Glossary

These commands are going to be able to be used with your Raspberry Pi to accomplish goals that you want with your Raspberry Pi board.

Apt- get

This code has two different parts. The first part is going to be for advanced packaging tool which tells the program which software packages it needs to manage, and these packages are already going to be installed on your Linux machine, it is going to work best with the Debian Linux machines. And since Raspbian is Debian, then you are going to be allowed to use apt- get.

The apt is going to be a process that will simplify how you manage the software that is on the UNIX computer system all by automating the retrieval, installation, and configuration of the software packages that are already on your Raspberry Pi board.

When this code first came out, it was known as "dependency hell" due to the fact that some of the packages that were being installed had to go through a manual installation process. It caused the user not to know what they were doing, thus causing them to make a mistake and not get everything installed as it was supposed to be.

Apt – get is commonly used with Raspberry Pi when you use the prefix sudo so that you have the proper permission.

When you want to renew your local files to ensure that they contain the newest packages that have changed, you will use apt- get update.

Apt- get upgrade is going to place the latest versions of the packages in your system if they are already installed and a new version is readily available to be put on your computer. If there are new releases that cannot be upgraded without additional steps, they are going to be left as they are so that you have to upgrade them on your own.

You will need to do the update code before you do the upgrade code so that you can see if any packages are in need of being updated.

Apt – get install

With this code, you are going to be able to install or upgrade the packages that are in need to be updated or installed onto your Raspberry Pi. This includes any packages that are dependent.

Cat

Your cat command is going to do multiple things. First off, the word cat stands for catenate which is going to connect multiple things in a series. This will be one of the most common uses that you are going to use cat for. You can also use cat for things like

- Joining a text file to another text file
- Showing text files in your command line
- Copying the text file into a new document.

Let us imagine that you are wanting to show a text file on the screen that you are working with, you are going to use cat and the file name.

Once this command has been executed, you are going to see the file on the screen. However, if your file is a large file, then some of the contents are going to be dumped so that they result in a scrolling waterfall of text on the screen just to ensure that everything is placed on the screen for you to see.

You also have the option of displaying two different files one right after the other with the cat command. You will use the same command that you used earlier, but you are going to add in the word bar so that they appear on your screen one after the other.

You do not necessarily have to have a file sent to your screen, you can also have that file forwarded to a different file, or we can rename that file with the cat command. You are going to use the same cat command that you have been using except now you are going to add in newfile.txt so that a new file is created from the file that you have selected.

This is essentially the same process as copy the file and redirecting it. However, if you want to take it a step further, you have the option of taking that file and combining it with the original file. So, your code is going to look something like this.

Cat file name. Txt bar. Txt > new file. Txt

Lastly, you have the option to use cat to append a file that already exists. In orde to do that, your code will look a little something like this.
Cat file name. Txt >> file that already exists. txt

The double arrow is going to redirect your operator so that it searches for the other file that you already have on your system to add the new file to it.

Please remember where it says file name, you are going to need to put the name of the file that you want to work. If you brought in a file name, you are going to receive and error message because the system is not going to know what file you want to work.

Conclusion

Thank you for making it through to the end of *Raspberry Pi 3*, let's hope it was informative and able to provide you with all of the tools you need to achieve your goals whatever it may be.

The next step is to use the information that you have learned in this book and get to coding with Raspberry Pi 3. You are going to be able to create a lot of projects that are going to improve your life so that it is easier.

Raspberry Pi 3 has a lot of potential to change the world; the proper people are going to have to be able to code with it. Therefore this book is meant to reach out to those that want to learn how to code with the board and use it.

Finally, if you found this book useful in any way, a review on Amazon is always appreciated!

Thank you and good luck.

Made in the USA
Middletown, DE
15 November 2017